SQL Server interview questions

Explain the use of keyword WITH ENCRYPTION. Create a Store Procedure with Encryption.

It is a way to convert the original text of the stored procedure into encrypted form. The stored procedure gets obfuscated and the output of this is not visible to

```
CREATE PROCEDURE Abc
WITH ENCRYPTION
AS
<<   SELECT statement>>
GO
```

What is a linked server in SQL Server?

It enables SQL server to address diverse data sources like OLE DB similarly. It allows Remote server access and has the ability to issue distributed queries, updates, commands and transactions.

Features and concepts of Analysis Services

Analysis Services is a middle tier server for analytical processing, OLAP, and Data mining. It manages multidimensional cubes of data and provides access to heaps of information including aggregation of data One can create data mining models from data sources and use it for Business Intelligence also including reporting features.

Some of the key features are:

- Ease of use with a lot of wizards and designers.
- Flexible data model creation and management
- Scalable architecture to handle OLAP
- Provides integration of administration tools, data sources, security, caching, and reporting etc.
- Provides extensive support for custom applications

What is Analysis service repository?

Every Analysis server has a repository to store metadata for the objects like cubes, data sources etc. It's by default stored in a MS Access database which can be also migrated to a SQL Server database.

What is SQL service broker?

Service Broker allows internal and external processes to send and receive guaranteed, asynchronous messaging. Messages can also be sent to remote servers hosting databases as well. The concept of queues is used by the broker to put a message in a queue and continue with other applications asynchronously. This enables client applications to process messages at their leisure without blocking the broker. Service Broker uses the concepts of message ordering, coordination, multithreading and receiver management to solve some major message queuing problems. It allows for loosely coupled services, for database applications.

What is user defined datatypes and when you should go for them?

User defined data types are based on system data types. They should be used when multiple tables need to store the same type of data in a column and you need to ensure that all these columns are exactly the same including length, and nullability.

Parameters for user defined datatype:

Name

System data type on which user defined data type is based upon.

Nullability.

For example, a user-defined data type called **post_code** could be created based on **char** system data type.

What is bit datatype?

A bit datatype is an integer data type which can store either a 0 or 1 or null value.

Describe the XML support SQL server extends.

SQL Server (server-side) supports 3 major elements:

a. Creation of XML fragments: This is done from the relational data using FOR XML to the select query.

b. Ability to shred xml data to be stored in the database.

c. Finally, storing the xml data.

Client-side XML support in SQL Server is in the form of SQLXML. It can be described in terms of

- **XML Views:** providing bidirectional mapping between XML schemas and relational tables.
- **Creation of XML Templates:** allows creation of dynamic sections in XML.

What is SQL Server English Query?

English query allows accessing the relational databases through English Query applications. Such applications permit the users to ask the database to fetch data based on simple English instead of using SQL statements.

What is the purpose of SQL Profiler in SQL server?

SQL profiler is a tool to monitor performance of various stored procedures. It is used to debug the queries and procedures. Based on performance, it identifies the slow executing queries. Capture any problems by capturing the events on production environment so that they can be solved.

What is XPath?

XPath is an expressions to select a xml node in an XML document.
It allows the navigation on the XML document to the straight to the element where we need to reach and access the attributes.

What are the Authentication Modes in SQL Server?

a. Windows Authentication Mode (Windows Authentication): uses user's Windows account
b. Mixed Mode (Windows Authentication and SQL Server Authentication): uses either windows or SQL server

Explain Data Definition Language, Data Control Language and Data Manipulation Language.

Data Definition Language (DDL):- are the SQL statements that define the database structure.
Example:

a. CREATE
b. ALTER
c. DROP
d. TRUNCATE
e. COMMENT
f. RENAME

Data Manipulation Language (DML):- statements are used for manipulate or edit data.
Example:

a. SELECT - retrieve data from the a database
b. INSERT - insert data into a table
c. UPDATE - updates existing data within a table
d. DELETE
e. MERGE
f. CALL
g. EXPLAIN PLAN
h. LOCK TABLE

Data Control Language (DCL):- statements to take care of the security and authorization.

Examples:

a. GRANT
b. REVOKE

What are the steps to process a single SELECT statement?

Steps

a. The select statement is broken into logical units
b. A sequence tree is built based on the keywords and expressions in the form of the logical units.
c. Query optimizer checks for various permutations and combinations to figure out the fastest way using minimum resources to access the source tables. The best found way is called as an execution plan.
d. Relational engine executes the plan and processes the data

Explain GO Command.

Go command is a signal to execute the entire batch of SQL statements after previous Go.

What is the significance of NULL value and why should we avoid permitting null values?

NULL value means that no entry has been made into the column. It states that the corresponding value is either unknown or undefined. It is different from zero or "". They should be avoided to avoid the complexity in select & update queries and also because columns

which have constraints like primary
or foreign key constraints cannot
contain a NULL value.

What is the difference between UNION and UNION ALL?

UNION selects only distinct values
whereas UNION ALL selects all
values and not just distinct ones.
UNION: SELECT column_names
FROM table_name1
UNION
SELECT column_names FROM
table_name2
UNION All: SELECT column_names
FROM table_name1

UNION ALL
SELECT column_names FROM
table_name2

What is use of DBCC Commands?

DBCC (Database consistency
checker) act as Database console
commands for SQL Server to check
database consistency. They are
grouped as:
Maintenance: Maintenance tasks on
Db, filegroup, index etc. Commands
include DBCC CLEANTABLE, DBCC
INDEXDEFRAG, DBCC DBREINDEX,
DBCC SHRINKDATABASE, DBCC
DROPCLEANBUFFERS, DBCC
SHRINKFILE, DBCC FREEPROCCACHE,
and DBCC UPDATEUSAGE.

Miscellaneous: Tasks such as enabling tracing, removing dll from memory. Commands include DBCC dllname, DBCC HELP, DBCC FREESESSIONCACHE, DBCC TRACEOFF, DBCC FREESYSTEMCACHE, and DBCC TRACEON.

Informational: Tasks which gather and display various types of information. Commands include DBCC INPUTBUFFER, DBCC SHOWCONTIG, DBCC OPENTRAN, DBCC SQLPERF, DBCC OUTPUTBUFFER, DBCC TRACESTATUS, DBCC PROCCACHE, DBCC USEROPTIONS, and DBCC SHOW_STATISTICS.

Validation: Operations for validating on Db, index, table etc. Commands include DBCC CHECKALLOC, DBCC CHECKFILEGROUP, DBCC CHECKCATALOG, DBCC CHECKIDENT, DBCC CHECKCONSTRAINTS, DBCC CHECKTABLE, and DBCC CHECKDB.

What is Log Shipping?

Log shipping defines the process for automatically taking backup of the database and transaction files on a SQL Server and then restoring them on a standby/backup server. This keeps the two SQL Server instances in sync with each other. In case production server fails, users simply need to be pointed to the standby/backup server. Log shipping primarily consists of 3 operations:

Backup transaction logs of the Production server.

Copy these logs on the standby/backup server.

Restore the log on standby/backup server.

What is the difference between a Local and a Global temporary table?

Temporary tables are used to allow short term use of data in SQL Server. They are of 2 types:

Local	Global
Only available to	Available to any

the current Db connection for current user and are cleared when connection is closed.	connection once created. They are cleared when the last connection is closed.
Multiple users can't share a local temporary table.	Can be shared by multiple user sessions.

What is the STUFF and how does it differ from the REPLACE function?

Both STUFF and REPLACE are used to replace characters in a string.

select replace('abcdef','ab','xx')
results in xxcdef

select replace('defdefdef','def','abc') results in abcabcabc
We cannot replace a specific occurrence of "def" using REPLACE.

select stuff('defdefdef',4, 3,'abc') results in defabcdef

where 4 is the character to begin replace from and 3 is the number of characters to replace.

What are the rules to use the ROWGUIDCOL property to define a globally unique identifier column?

Only one column can exist per table that is attached with ROWGUIDCOL property. One can then use

$ROWGUID instead of column name in select list.

What is the actions prevented once referential integrity is enforced?

Actions prevented are:

- Breaking of relationships is prevented once referential integrity on a database is enforced.
- Can't delete a row from primary table if there are related rows in secondary table.
- Can't update primary table's primary key if row being modified has related rows in secondary table.

- Can't insert a new row in secondary table if there are not related rows in primary table.
- Can't update secondary table's foreign key if there is no related row in primary table.

What are the commands available for Summarizing Data in SQL Server?

Commands for summarizing data in SQL Server:

Command	Description	Syntax/Example
SUM	Sums related values	SELECT SUM(Sal) as Tot from

		Table1;
AVG	Average value	SELECT AVG(Sal) as Avg_Sal from Table1;
COUNT	Returns number of rows of resultset	SELECT COUNT(*) from Table1;
MAX	Returns max value from a resultset	SELECT MAX(Sal) from Table1;
MIN	Returns min value from a resultset	SELECT MIN(Sal) from Table1;
GROUP BY	Arrange	SELECT ZIP,City

	resultset in groups	FROM Emp GROUP BY ZIP
ORDER BY	Sort resultset	SELECT ZIP,City FROM Emp ORDER BY City

List out the difference between CUBE operator and ROLLUP operator

Difference between CUBE and ROLLUP:

CUBE	ROLLUP
It's an additional switch to GROUP BY clause. It can	It's an extension to GROUP BY clause. It's used to

be applied to all aggregation functions to return cross tabular result sets. .	extract statistical and summarized information from result sets. It creates groupings and then applies aggregation functions on them.
Produces all possible combinations of subtotals specified in GROUP BY clause and a Grand Total.	Produces only some possible subtotal combinations.

What are the guidelines to use bulk copy utility of SQL Server?

Bulk copy is an API that allows interacting with SQL Server to export/import data in one of the two data formats. Bulk copy needs sufficient system credentials.

- Need INSERT permissions on destination table while importing.
- Need SELECT permissions on source table while exporting.
- Need SELECT permissions on sysindexes, sysobjects and syscolumns tables.

bcp.exe northwind..cust out "c:\cust.txt" –c -T

Export all rows in Northwind.Cust table to an ASCII-character formatted text file.

What are the capabilities of Cursors?

Capabilities of cursors:
- Cursor reads every row one by one.
- Cursors can be used to update a set of rows or a single specific row in a resultset
- Cursors can be positioned to specific rows.
- Cursors can be parameterized and hence are flexible.
- Cursors lock row(s) while updating them.

What are the ways to controlling Cursor Behavior?

There are 2 ways to control Cursor behavior:

- Cursor Types: Data access behavior depends on the type of cursor; forward only, static, keyset-drive and dynamic.
- Cursor behaviors: Keywords such as SCROLL and INSENSITIVE along with the Cursor declaration define scrollability and sensitivity of the cursor.

What are the advantages of using Stored Procedures?

Advantages of using stored procedures are:

- They are easier to maintain and troubleshoot as they are modular.
- Stored procedures enable better tuning for performance.
- Using stored procedures is much easier from a GUI end than building/using complex queries.
- They can be part of a separate layer which allows separating the concerns. Hence Database layer can be handled by separate developers proficient in database queries.
- Help in reducing network usage.

- Provides more scalability to an application.
- Reusable and hence reduce code.

What are the ways to code efficient transactions?

Some ways and guidelines to code efficient transactions:
- Do not ask for an input from a user during a transaction.
- Get all input needed for a transaction before starting the transaction.
- Transaction should be atomic
- Transactions should be as short and small as possible.

- Rollback a transaction if a user intervenes and re-starts the transaction.
- Transaction should involve a small amount of data as it needs to lock the number of rows involved.
- Avoid transactions while browsing through data.

What are the differences among batches, stored procedures, and triggers?

Batch	Stored Procedure	Triggers
Collection	It's a	It's a type

| or group of SQL statements. All statements of a batch are compiled into one executional unit called execution plan. All statements are then executed statement by statement. | collection or group of SQL statements that's compiled once but used many times. | of Stored procedure that cannot be called directly. Instead it fires when a row is updated, deleted, or inserted. |

What security features are available for stored procedures?

Security features for stored procedures:
- Grants users permissions to execute a stored procedure irrespective of the related tables.
- Grant users users permission to work with a stored procedure to access a restricted set of data yet no give them permissions to update or select underlying data.
- Stored procedures can be granted execute permissions rather than setting permissions on data itself.

- Provide more granular security control through stored procedures rather than complete control on underlying data in tables.

What are the instances when triggers are appropriate?

Scenarios for using triggers:
- To create a audit log of database activity.
- To apply business rules.
- To apply some calculation on data from tables which is not stored in them.
- To enforce referential integrity.

- Alter data in a third party application
- To execute SQL statements as a result of an event/condition automatically.

What are the restrictions applicable while creating views?

Restrictions applicable while creating views:

- A view cannot be indexed.
- A view cannot be Altered or renamed. Its columns cannot be renamed.
- To alter a view, it must be dropped and re-created.

- ANSI_NULLS and QUOTED_IDENTIFIER options should be turned on to create a view.
- All tables referenced in a view must be part of the same database.
- Any user defined functions referenced in a view must be created with SCHEMABINDING option.
- Cannot use ROWSET, UNION, TOP, ORDER BY, DISTINCT, COUNT(*), COMPUTE, COMPUTE BY in views.

What are the events recorded in a transaction log?

Events recorded in a transaction log:

- Broker event category includes events produced by Service Broker.
- Cursors event category includes cursor operations events.
- CLR event category includes events fired by .Net CLR objects.
- Database event category includes events of data.log files shrinking or growing on their own.
- Errors and Warning event category includes SQL Server warnings and errors.
- Full text event category include events occurred when text searches are started, interrupted, or stopped.

- Locks event category includes events caused when a lock is acquired, released, or cancelled.
- Object event category includes events of database objects being created, updated or deleted.
- OLEDB event category includes events caused by OLEDB calls.
- Performance event category includes events caused by DML operators.
- Progress report event category includes Online index operation events.
- Scans event category includes events notifying table/index scanning.
- Security audit event category includes audit server activities.

- Server event category includes server events.
- Sessions event category includes connecting and disconnecting events of clients to SQL Server.
- Stored procedures event category includes events of execution of Stored procedures.
- Transactions event category includes events related to transactions.
- TSQL event category includes events generated while executing TSQL statements.
- User configurable event category includes user defined events.

Describe when checkpoints are created in a transaction log.

Activities causing checkpoints are:
- When a checkpoint is explicitly executed.
- A logged operation is performed on the database.
- Database files have been altered using Alter Database command.
- SQL Server has been stopped explicitly or on its own.
- SQL Server periodically generates checkpoints.
- Backup of a database is taken.

Define Truncate and Delete commands.

TRUNCATE	DELETE
This is also a logged operation but in terms of deallocation of data pages.	This is a logged operation for every row.
Cannot TRUNCATE a table that has foreign key constraints.	Any row not violating a constraint can be Deleted.
Resets identity column to the default starting value.	Does not reset the identity column. Starts where it left from last.
Removes all rows from a table.	Used delete all or selected rows

	from a table based on WHERE clause.
Cannot be Rolled back.	Need to Commit or Rollback
DDL command	DML command

Desktop:

Start Menu : Windows Logo (or) Ctrl + ESC

My computer : Windows Logo + E

New Folder : Ctrl + Shift + N

Switching Through Applications : Alt + Tab

Switching Through Applications without always hitting alt + Tab : Ctrl + Alt + Tab

Switch through open applicatons :
Alt + tab (or) Windows Logo +Tab
(aero effect in windows7)
Switching through applications in
aero mode : **Ctrl + Windows Logo
+Tab** & use mouse to croll.
Switch focus between applications :
Alt + ESC
Run : Windows Logo +R
Desktop : Windows Logo + D
Minimize all windows : Windows
Logo + M
Restore all minimized windows :
Windows Logo + Shift + M
Flip window to left / Right :
Windows Logo + Left arrow/Right
arrow
Lock Screen : Windows Logo + L
System Properties : Windows Logo
+Pause

Adding different Monitors :
Windows Logo + P
Close a window : Alt + F4 (or) Ctrl +
W
Full Screen : F11
Task Manager : Ctrl + Alt + Del (or)
Ctrl + Shift + ESC
Minimize window : Alt + Spacebar
& then **N**
Close window : Alt + Spacebar &
then **C**
Restore window : Alt + Spacebar &
then **R**
Copy,Cut,Paste : Ctrl + C,X,V
Rename File / Folder : F2
Browser:
New Tab : Ctrl + T
Go to address bar : Ctrl + L (or) Alt
+ D (or) F6
Switch between tabs : Ctrl + Tab /
Ctrl + Shift + Tab

Go to nth tab : Ctrl + 1,2,3,...9
Search for keyword : Ctrl + F / F3
Downloads : Ctrl + J
History : Ctrl + H
Clear History Page : Ctrl + Shift + Del
View Original size of page : Ctrl + 0(zero)
Zoom in or out web page : Ctrl + '+' Ctrl + '-'
Bookmark a web page : Ctrl + D
Directly go to GOOGLE.COM : **www.google.com/ncr**
Refresh Page : F5 (or) Ctrl + R
Go back / forward : Alt + Left / Right arrow
Open a file in your computer : Ctrl + **O**
Browse one page down/up : Spacebar / Shift + Spacebar
Developer Tools : F12

Open Source code : Ctrl + U

http://praveenshandilya.blogspot.in/

www.ingramcontent.com/pod-product-compliance
Lightning Source LLC
Chambersburg PA
CBHW041146050326
40689CB00001B/508